Health and My Body

Care for Your Body

by Martha E. H. Rustad

PEBBLE
a capstone imprint

Pebble Explore is published by Pebble, an imprint of Capstone
1710 Roe Crest Drive
North Mankato, Minnesota 56003
www.capstonepub.com

**Library of Congress Cataloging-in-Publication Data is available on
the Library of Congress website.**
ISBN: 978-1-9771-2389-3 (library binding)
ISBN: 978-1-9771-2689-4 (paperback)
ISBN: 978-1-9771-2426-5 (eBook PDF)

Summary: From exercising to getting enough sleep, you are in charge
of your body. It's important to take good care of it. Learn simple ways
to keep your body healthy.

Image Credits
iStockphoto: FatCamera, 5; Shutterstock: 3445128471, 23, Africa
Studio, 15, 17, CC7, 19, Creativa Images, 27, gorillaimages, Cover,
karelnoppe, 10, Lana K, 20, Lilya Espinosa, 21, Lotus_studio, 7,
michaeljung, 25, Monkey Business Images, 6, New Africa, spread
12-13, NicoleMorley, 9, nortongo, 8, photonova, design element,
Pressmaster, 26, Rawpixel.com, 11, Sergey Novikov, 29, worawit_j, 24

Editorial Credits
Editor: Christianne Jones; Designer: Sarah Bennett; Media Researcher:
Morgan Walters; Production Specialist: Laura Manthe

Table of Contents

Bold words are in the glossary.

The Amazing Body

Your body is amazing. You have 206 bones. Your heart pumps blood through your entire body in about one minute. Your feet have about 500,000 sweat **glands**. The list goes on and on.

Everyone gets just one body. You need to take good care of it. Eat healthy foods. Stay active. Get enough sleep. Help your body stay healthy so it can stay amazing.

Healthy Choices

Take care of your body by eating well. Start off the day with a healthy breakfast. Choose healthy foods all day.

At each meal, look at your plate. About half should be fruits and vegetables. They have the **vitamins** your body needs to grow.

About one fourth of your plate should be whole grains. Whole grains include brown rice and whole wheat pasta. The last fourth of your plate should be protein. Protein includes beans, meat, and nuts.

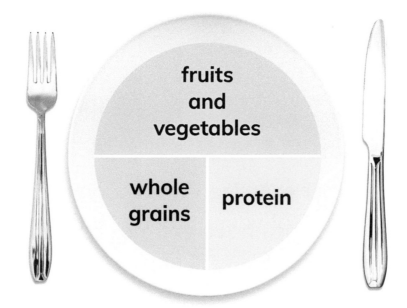

fruits
and
vegetables

whole
grains

protein

More than half of your body is made of water. Your body needs water to keep all its parts working. Drink extra water after exercise. Avoid soda and fruit juice. They have extra sugar that your body doesn't need.

Choose healthy snacks. Mix yogurt with berries. Dip veggies in hummus. Eat a cheese stick or some nuts.

Sweets are yummy. But too much sugar is not good for your body. Limit sweet choices. You can still have dessert. Just make it a small piece and enjoy every bite.

Move Your Body!

Exercise will help you grow and stay strong. Get about an hour of exercise every day. Make your muscles work. Your heart should be pumping. Your lungs should be working hard.

Play at the park. Start a game of tag with your friends. Take turns being it. Go on a hike. Spot different plants. Listen for animal noises. Look for animal tracks.

After exercise, take time to stretch. Reach up high and down low. Feel your muscles getting longer. Let your body relax. Take a few deep breaths. Your heartbeat slows down.

It's fun to watch TV or play video games. But being healthy means you should limit your screen time. It's not good for your eyes. And it's not good for your body to sit for too long.

Recharge

Take care of your body by resting it every night. Sleep is important for your brain. It gives your brain time to recharge. Kids need between 10 and 12 hours of sleep each night.

Your body needs sleep. At night, your body makes certain **chemicals**. They keep you healthy. They also help you grow. If you don't sleep your body will get run down.

Pick a bedtime with your family. Keep the same bedtime every night, even on weekends and during the summer. Get up at about the same time each day too.

Plan a bedtime routine that helps you relax. About an hour before bed turn off all electronics. Read a book or take a bath. Turn off some lights. These actions tell your body it is time to go to sleep.

Keeping Clean

Take care of your body by keeping it clean. Dirt and **germs** stick to your skin. Germs can make you sick.

Wash your hands after using the bathroom. Wash before and after you eat too. It seems simple, but it's easy to forget. Use soap and scrub for 20 seconds. That's about as long as singing the "Happy Birthday" song twice.

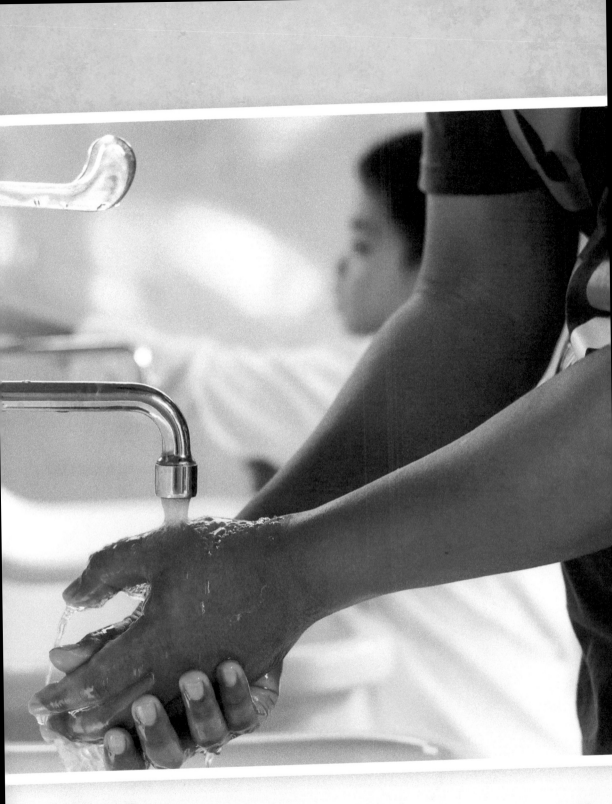

Everyone gets stinky. You have tiny holes in your skin called sweat glands. They let out sweat. Sweat helps keeps your body cool. But it can smell bad.

Kids should take a warm bath or shower a few times a week. Wash your hair. Scrub your body with soap. Be sure to clean under your arms. Put on clean clothes. You will smell and feel fresh!

Your teeth are very important. You need them to eat, smile, and talk. But germs can cause tiny holes in teeth. The holes are called **cavities**.

Brush your teeth twice each day. Clean them in the morning and before bed. Use a soft toothbrush. Use toothpaste that has **fluoride**. Fluoride is good for teeth.

Brush for about two minutes. Brush the top and sides of each tooth. Use floss between your teeth.

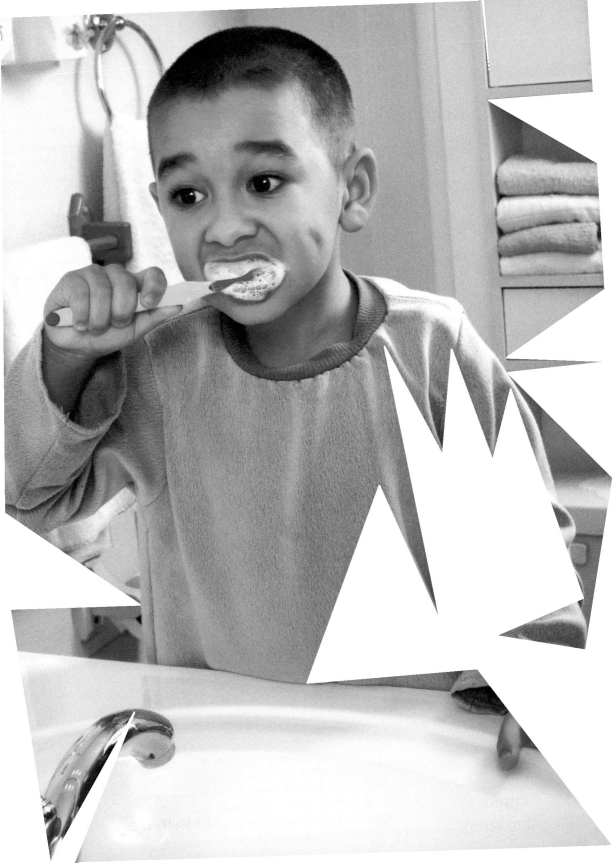

Dentists and Doctors

Dentists and doctors help you take care of yourself. Dentists take care of teeth. Visit your dentist twice a year.

A dental **hygienist** cleans your teeth. They scrape off yellow gunk that sticks to teeth. It is called **plaque**. It can lead to cavities.

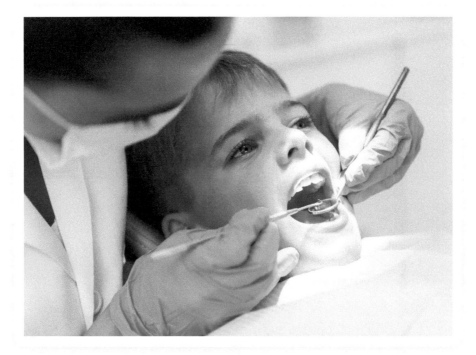

The dentist looks at X-rays of your teeth. X-rays are special pictures of the inside of your body.

Doctors help you take care of your body. They help you when you feel sick. You also visit them for checkups. A nurse checks your height and weight. They look at how you are growing.

Doctors also give shots called **immunizations**. These shots give you a tiny bit of a germ. Your body fights the germ. This keeps your body from getting really sick.

Lots of people help you stay healthy, but you must keep your body safe.

Wear a helmet when you ride your bike. This protects your brain. Use a seat belt in the car. This will protect your body in a crash. Look up when you are walking. Don't look down at your phone. You could trip or run into something.

You are in charge of your body. You need to take good care of it. It's the only one you get!

Glossary

cavity (KA-vuh-tee)—a hole in a tooth caused by decay, or rotting

chemical (KE-muh-kuhl)—a basic substance that makes up all materials

fluoride (FLOOR-ide)—a mineral put on teeth to make them stronger and prevent cavities

germ (JURM)—a small living thing that causes disease

gland (GLAND)—an organ in the body that makes certain chemicals

hygienist (hye-JEN-ist)—a person who is trained to help the dentist; hygienists clean teeth and take X-rays

immunization (i-MYOON-uh-zay-shun)—a shot with a tiny bit of a germ in it; this shot keeps you from getting sick

plaque (PLAK)—a thick, yellow substance that sticks to teeth

vitamin (VYE-tuh-min)—a part of food that helps your body stay healthy

Read More

Arnez, Lynda. *We Stay Healthy*. New York: Gareth Stevens, 2020.

Holmes, Kirsty. *My Health*. New York: Crabtree, 2019.

Schuette, Sarah L. *Health Safety*. North Mankato, MN: Pebble, 2020.

Internet Sites

Be a Fit Kid
https://kidshealth.org/en/kids/fit-kid.html?WT

Choose My Plate
https://www.choosemyplate.gov/kids

How to Brush Your Teeth Properly
https://safeYouTube.net/w/cPxr

Index